GOING, GOING, GONE!

MUSIC AND MEMORIES FROM BROADCAST BASEBALL

The Life, Times, & Music™ Series

Acknowledgments

I would be remiss if I did not thank my parents, Dr. Rocco and Barbara—
they are my link to the generations that lived before television dominated
our social, political, and intellectual landscape.

Thanks also to Ben Boyington and Nathaniel Marunas—you two
should get out and enjoy yourselves more often. And finally, thanks to my
two favorite Texans: Andrew Hager and Susan Choi.

GOING, GOING, GONE!

MUSIC AND MEMORIES FROM BROADCAST BASEBALL

The Life, Times, & Music™ Series

Anthony De Simone

Friedman/Fairfax
Publishers

A FRIEDMAN GROUP BOOK

Copyright © 1994 by Michael Friedman Publishing Group, Inc.

ISBN 1-56799-084-3

THE LIFE, TIMES, & MUSIC ™ *SERIES: GOING, GOING, GONE!*
Music and Memories from Broadcast Baseball
was prepared and produced by
Michael Friedman Publishing Group, Inc.
15 West 26th Street
New York, New York 10010

Editor: Benjamin Boyington
Art Director: Jeff Batzli
Designer: Lori Thorn
Photography Researcher: Emilya Naymark

Cover Photography Credits: Yankee Stadium: FPG International;
Grass: Warren Schultz; Joe DiMaggio: National Baseball Library, Cooperstown, N.Y.;
Baseball and Glove: © Cezus/FPG International;
Abbott and Costello: Movie Star News; Red Barber: Archive Photos

Printed in the United States of America

For bulk purchases and special sales, please contact:
Friedman/Fairfax Publishers
15 West 26th Street
New York, NY 10010
(212) 685-6610   FAX (212) 685-1307

Contents

The Dawn of Radio Baseball

I n 1920 a new player came up to bat—"wireless telegraphy," which we know today as radio. On November 2, 1920, station KDKA in Pittsburgh, Pennsylvania, built, owned, and operated by the Westinghouse Company, aired its first "broadcast." This marked the dawn of a new era, not only in the realm of communications, but also in the world of baseball.

On the afternoon of August 5, 1921, Harold Arlin, a foreman at Westinghouse, set up his equipment behind the home plate screen at Forbes Field (Pittsburgh) and broadcast the game between the Phillies and the Pirates over pioneer sending station KDKA. Because the popularity and avail-ability of the radio were still in their earliest stages, it is unknown how many people heard this first baseball broadcast. Regardless of the number of listeners, the rally was on. Just as a walk is as good as a hit, Arlin's attempt, however modest and primitive, allowed the big hitters to come up to bat.

Radio expanded baseball from a "pastime" to a multimillion-dollar industry, inspired amateur "hams" to invent the telecommunications industry, and entertained the world.

Harold Arlin

Above: Station KDKA on November 2, 1920. The broadcasting of professional baseball over the radio was met with skepticism by some pioneers. Below: Harold Arlin standing at the microphone in 1921.

A Westinghouse foreman during the day, Harold Arlin spent evenings in the KDKA studio broadcasting various events. In 1921, at the age of twenty-six, this native of Illinois engineered the first broadcast of a professional baseball game, and the echoes of his experiment can be heard more clearly today than ever before.

He was a pioneer who was responsible for many "firsts" in broadcasting history. On August 6, 1921, for example, he broadcast the first tennis match. And on October 19 of the same year, he called the first football game broadcast over the radio: University of Pittsburgh versus University of West Virginia.

The move from studio broadcasting to airing the game from the ballpark was an experiment that, to Arlin, occurred in the natural chain of events. He had been the first to include updates of baseball news from the station's studio during his "program."

Ironically, Arlin did not see radio broadcasting of baseball as becoming a giant industry. Quite the contrary—he doubted the mixture of radio and baseball as a commercially successful venture. After about six years in broadcasting, he moved into corporate relations.

Arlin and crew combated primitive technology, crowd noise, faulty and unreliable transmitting equipment, and a host of unforeseeable complications in order to launch their broadcasts. He has left us with a charming testament to the naive days of the early twenties.

Radio Baseball Gets on Base

The first commercial station, KDKA, was soon followed by northeastern stations WJZ (Newark, New Jersey) and WBZ (Springfield, Massachusetts). These stations were linked by their affiliation with the Westinghouse Network. The year 1921 also ushered in the first broadcast of a World Series game—between

the New York Giants and the Yankees. The best-of-nine Series took place at, and was aired exclusively from, the Polo Grounds (Manhattan). Grantland Rice, a reporter for the *New York Herald Tribune*, had a direct line from the Polo Grounds to KDKA. Game one, the only game broadcast during the 1921 Series, ended in a 3–0 victory for the Yankees.

Grantland Rice called the first World Series game broadcast over the radio.

WJZ and WBZ were out of range of the signal on which Rice was being broadcast, but they salvaged the situation by broadcasting the first baseball "re-creation." A reporter from the *Newark Call* relayed the events via telephone from the Polo Grounds to the top of the Newark Westinghouse Building. There, thirty-seven-year-old Tommy Cowan pieced together the game and delivered the play-by-play to the local listen-

The Giants won the 1921 Series (shown above) as well as the 1922 Classic, but the Yankees' thirty-year dynasty and the era of Babe Ruth were under way.

*Frankie Frisch slides safely into third base in the 1922 Series. Many fans listened to
that year's October Classic on the Aeriola Sr. vacuum-tube radio, which sold for
about twenty-five dollars.*

ers. He had no scorecard, no spotters, no rosters, no statistics—all he had to
work with were his intuition and his imagination. Though his product was
rough around the edges, Cowan soon secured for himself the position of first
broadcast hero of the East.

Although there was no way to estimate the precise number of listeners, the feedback from baseball fans who had heard Arlin's pioneering
baseball broadcast was overwhelmingly positive. A newspaper article of the
day speculated that more than three million American homes were outfitted
with a radio. The media blitz was already upon the urban population, and
the people responsible for broadcasting had—at best—only one or two
years' experience with the medium. Broadcasters quickly became caught up
in the passionate response to the novelty of radio baseball and the excitement it was generating.

The last best-of-nine Series was played in 1922, and it was a repeat
of the 1921 battle between the Giants and Yankees at the Polo Grounds. This
was the first repeat Series since 1908, when the Cubs and Tigers had fought
it out for the second year in a row. Unlike in 1921, however, this time the entire Series was broadcast.

Once again, Newark station WJZ was linked to the Polo Grounds.
The chief engineer at WJZ, Charles W. Horn, cajoled Western Union's vice
president, J.C. Williver, into leasing his company's wires to the station.

Through Newark's transmitter, Grantland Rice, teamed with writer
W.B. McGheehan and engineer Raymond F. Guy, described the opening game to
an estimated audience of five million. The crowd at the Polo Grounds was

What Is a Network?

Radio broadcasting is based on a central transmitter that broadcasts program sequences to a multitude of individual receivers. Programs are often produced centrally and then distributed through a network of local stations via wire or a more sophisticated microwave link. In the early days of radio, the problem of transmitting weak signals over large distances forced stations to form networks.

Radio stations are equipped with extremely large antennae that are able to receive many transmissions that home radios

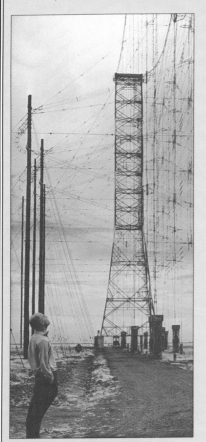

In the first half of the twentieth century, baseball was professional sports, and sports soon became media. Radio was a link shared by all Americans, a link that would provide the nation with uniform ideas and interests.

are unable to pick up. Most simply stated, a network is a series of sending stations owned and operated as a unit that work together in selecting a program format. Each of these stations has access to signals that originate with the network, and the broadcast rights and benefits are shared by the networked stations.

By 1924, networking had become complicated because of copyright laws that restricted the use of programs. Local stations were abundant, but by 1927, NBC and CBS dominated radio because they had the financial resources to consistently bring national and even international news to their audience. (These two "controlling" networks were accused by many of violating antitrust laws.) World Series coverage, for example, was a networking jubilee.

The Federal Radio Act (FRA) of 1927 was a congressional control measure that assigned a specific band of frequency to each individual station and determined the station's wattage. In 1934, the FRA evolved into the Federal Communications Commission (FCC), which for the most part has governed both radio and television since. Both of these acts were designed to regulate existing networks and stations. The technological innovations that resulted in the expansion of networks were almost always bought by NBC or CBS in an effort to consolidate their control.

In the twenties, listening audiences were delighted by the "exotic" programs brought to them by the networks. Local stations welcomed the security of operating through networks because quality programming is expensive to produce, and sponsors quickly began promoting products through national networks, thus reaping tremendous profits. Almost overnight, networking transformed the radio industry into the most powerful media tool on the planet.

Graham McNamee (standing, with binoculars) set the standards for the broadcasting industry.

approximately forty thousand, and their roar could be heard over the radio. Because of the close proximity of the broadcasters' setup to the field, the umpire's calls, the players' comments, and even the conversations of those sitting near the announcer were audible. One must keep in mind that there was no announcer's booth at that time. The announcer sat in a box seat, with the fans, and spoke into "carbon" microphones or telephone receivers with the earpiece sawed off. This setup certainly didn't look pretty, but it worked.

Stations WGY in Schenectady, New York, and WBZ in Springfield, Massachusetts, were linked to WJZ via cable, and thus were able to relay the broadcast of the 1922 Series to listeners in their areas. With this network in place, the listening audience was not limited to the area around WJZ in western Pennsylvania—much of the northeastern section of the country was able to receive the games.

Because he was a journalist, Rice knew there was an audience—sports fans had been following the daily and weekly successes of their teams through newspaper box scores for years. It was logical for Rice to conclude that radio broadcasts scooped the headlines from the next edition as well as cut fans in on the action. Arlin and Rice were the perfect "one-two" hitters in the radio baseball lineup. They were lightweight and didn't swing too hard; they got on base; and they were fast, moving quickly in order to stir up a rally, never overestimating their own power but instead deferring to those who followed them in the order to knock them home. Fortunately for them, in the "on-deck circle," and swinging a big bat, was a man named Graham McNamee—and boy, could he clear the bases.

In September of 1923, McNamee was slated as Grantland Rice's "color man" for the World Series, the first to be broadcast on a nationwide radio network. His job was to talk about the crowd, celebrities, and general atmosphere at the game, filling in the dead air between innings. Rice, a newspaper man and top bill for the Series broadcast, abdicated his position as caller of the Series after the fourth inning of game three, because of monotony. McNamee assumed Rice's role for the rest of the Series broadcast and described Ruth's three home runs, Bob Meusel's eight runs batted in, Frankie Frisch's vacuumlike fielding and .400 batting average, and finally, Casey Stengel's legendary inside-the-park home run.

Graham McNamee

The word *broadcast* was originally an agricultural term referring to the scattering of seed over a broad-based area rather than in neatly designated rows. McNamee was the first true "broadcaster"—all those who have followed are deeply indebted to him. His seed landed on the fertile soil of America's ears and its imagination. His career is a handrail that guides one through the early history of radio. Graham McNamee was born in 1889 in Washington, D.C. After his parents were divorced, young Graham moved with his mother to New York City. He studied piano and at age eighteen began singing lessons that would culminate in a modest career as a baritone. He received encouraging reviews by both the *New York Sun* and the *Times* for his stage performances, but was less than content with his achievement.

In May of 1923, on a break from jury duty at the federal court in Manhattan, McNamee walked in, unannounced, to station WEAF on Broadway. After a brief tour of the facilities, the charismatic young man of thirty-four was hired on the spot. His salary was thirty dollars a week, and his duties included broadcasts of all types.

McNamee would cover any event available or suitable for broadcasting. His first major assignment was in August of 1923; the WEAF management simply pointed him in the direction of the middleweight title bout between Harry Greb and Johnny Wilson and told him to broadcast it. Although he had no inside information and was not a boxing enthusiast, McNamee was a success because of his voice and style.

Initially based in New York City, McNamee gained fame overnight, and later became NBC's most notable radio personality. He traveled frequently and worked most of the "national" broadcasts, the largest, of course, being the World Series.

McNamee not only interviewed celebrities, but also announced opera performances, foreign coronations, and the Republican and Democratic conventions of 1924 (the Democratic convention lasted fourteen days), among other important events. All radio broadcasting at this time was performed live, with virtually no preparation. At first, no one gave much thought to what McNamee was doing—but single-handedly he was demonstrating the appeal and power one man could exercise over a nation.

It is significant that famed broadcaster Red Barber dedicated his book *The Broadcasters* to McNamee. The development of radio broadcasting as a respectable, reputable, professional vocation stems from McNamee's appeal as more than a figure put on the air simply to entertain. He recognized that his popularity was enormous and his impact profound. It cannot be overstated that McNamee's rise to fame occurred overnight. He broke into radio as radio was breaking into American culture. In 1923, he covered a championship prize fight, the World Series, and President Coolidge's message to Congress with the skill of an experienced veteran, but the field was as green as he was.

McNamee's appeal was personal and universal. His voice was soothing, melodic, and rich in character, and his tone was honest. He did not attempt to conceal any information from the public, because his intention was to "converse" with his audience. When he laughed on air, the nation smiled because his candor was genuine. It is no exaggeration to conclude that the initial popularity of baseball on the radio is due to McNamee's success. He was not competing with the demands of an industry in his first two years because there was no industry.

In all, McNamee called twelve World Series (from 1923 through 1934). Throughout his career, policemen would stop traffic and direct his car through, waving him on with a smile.

His dominance in his field brought the wrath of newspaper writers upon him. The reporters clearly saw the threat that McNamee, with his instant reporting, posed to their business.

In his broadcasts, McNamee was honest and unapologetic about the errors he would make. And it is, of course, understandable that he would make errors—given his schedule, it's amazing how few there were. Reporters and rivals alike would often defame his dependability. Ring Lardner, a journalist of the era, joked about his confusion over which game to write about, the one he saw at the Polo Grounds or the one he heard McNamee announce in the seat next to him. During the broad-

cast of the 1929 World Series, a reporter near McNamee was heard yelling, "McNamee, will you please pipe down?"

Graham McNamee died in May of 1942, at the age of fifty-three, of a brain embolism. McNamee had brought unfettered enthusiasm and unswerving dedication to his field, and although his career lasted only nineteen years, he set the standards for a new industry. He signed on with "Good evening, ladies and gentlemen of the radio audience," and signed off by saying, "This is Graham McNamee speaking. Good night, all." McNamee's coverage of ten sports, not to mention the assortment of other oddball events, without any time for him to prepare, was nothing short of brilliant. The announcers we hear today on radio or television would beg for mercy if they had a schedule that resembled McNamee's in even the slightest way. Graham McNamee stands as an American icon—the greatest broadcaster there ever was.

The Giants score a run in the 1923 Series. That year marked the first Series played at Yankee Stadium and Babe Ruth's first victory as a Yankee.

It must have been incredible for McNamee to sit in his box seat and think that people all over the nation were listening to *him* describe the events at the park—just five months before the Series, he hadn't even been in the radio business!

The attendance for the 1923 Series was 301,430—a record at the time. The Series ended on October 15, a Monday, with the Yankees beating the Giants four games to two. By Saturday, more than seventeen hundred letters had been sent to station WEAF, care of Graham McNamee—staggering numbers for that or any time. Considering the relative scarcity of radios at the time, and the novelty of the medium, McNamee's popularity was amazing. McNamee's career as a broadcaster would revolutionize radio within American society.

Today, radio and television programming are governed by sponsors and federal regulatory bodies, and as a consequence, all of the airtime is scheduled; there is a lack of free time on the air. Sponsors and network executives pay too much to lose even a nanosecond of their promotional airtime.

The broadcasting world McNamee knew was the inverse of today's. He would go on the air with little to no preparation and remain on—live—for hours on end. He was a one-man band, ad-libbing to an unknown but devoted audience. His style, characterized by a smooth, confident delivery, eased the audience into acceptance of the medium into their homes. McNamee seduced the country. Most importantly, McNamee represents the thread that sews together all elements of the time. Judge Kenesaw Mountain Landis, the first and most powerful Commissioner of Baseball, had tremendous respect for McNamee due to the massive appeal McNamee brought the game. Because of McNamee's role as spokesman for the World Series (the only baseball event that received radio attention at this early stage), the Commissioner concluded that the broadcaster was as powerful an ally as baseball could have.

If there is any correlation between power and popularity, then McNamee embodied it. In 1925, McNamee announced his third World Series and subsequently received more than fifty thousand letters and telegrams. (To understand these numbers a bit better, consider that when Red Barber was fired by the Yankees in the fall of 1966 he received about 250 letters—and felt that was a positive show of support from fans.) Ready or not, the big numbers were beginning to appear, and radio was not even five years old.

The Networks

By the early 1920s, sending stations had begun springing up throughout the country, broadcasting news, variety shows, music, and sporting events. AT&T was in the broadcasting business almost from the very beginning; also involved were RCA, Westinghouse, and General Electric. In 1922, WEAF New York, a child of AT&T, sold its first airtime to the Queensboro Corporation, a New York City realty company. The fees were one hundred dollars for ten minutes during the evening and fifty dollars for a ten-minute daytime spot.

David Sarnoff created the prototypical network, NBC.

The notion of inviting sponsors into the traffic of broadcasting was met initially with skepticism and apprehension. In the words of U.S. Department of Commerce Secretary Herbert Hoover, it was "inconceivable that we should allow so great a possibility for service...to be drowned in advertising chatter." Hoover ultimately ate his words and gave his blessing to commercial advertising, which rapidly became the dominant source of revenue for the networks. The thinking of the twenties was concerned with the underlying foundation of the broadcasting industry. Initially, the large companies, such as RCA, anticipated that their profits would come from the sales of radios, and the broadcast fees and subsequent expenses would be subsidized, or paid for outright, by the sales of these individual units. In hindsight, this seems ridiculous, but before the birth of commercial programming, the debate must have been ferocious.

NBC was formed as the result of a settlement between RCA and AT&T, and it began broadcasting formally on November 15, 1926. By January of 1927, NBC had split into the "Blue," which concentrated on public affairs programming, and the "Red," which aired music and comedy. WEAF was the main feed of the "Red," while WJZ fed the "Blue." The brain behind the NBC monster was David Sarnoff.

CBS went on air about ten months after NBC did so, in September of 1927. In the first year or two, CBS was teetering on the edge of bankruptcy. In September of 1928, the Congress Cigar Company, owned by the Paley family, bought the network after realizing that its cigar sales had jumped significantly after the firm had bought advertising time on local station WCAU. Young William S. Paley took the helm of CBS and turned it into the huge success it is today.

In 1943, by order of the Federal Communications Commission (FCC), NBC sold its "Blue" network. This resulted in the birth of ABC.

William Paley took CBS from bankruptcy to empire.

Ted Husing (left) and Les Quailey (right) were always pushing sports coverage to become more informative, accurate, and efficient.

As radio became more popular, people began to sit about the house, in the street, perhaps even in a car (it is said that traffic on the street in some towns would come to a halt when a game was on so that all could listen), and do something we take for granted—they would listen to a game and let their imaginations run wild with the exploits of the players.

Ted Husing arrived on the radio scene in September of 1924, winning an announcing position at WJZ, which by this time had moved its operations to New York. Husing was awarded the position after beating out 619 applicants who had responded to an advertisement run by the station. McNamee had achieved fame, and Husing's ambition was, in part, fueled by a desire to outdo McNamee.

At the time, radio stations regularly ran auditions, searching for new talent to fill the airwaves. With experienced announcers coming from all over the country, hoping to find a new and better position, the competition was fierce.

Husing opted to skip college and go directly into broadcasting. He worked in Washington at station WRC and in New York at WHN, and then moved to Boston in 1927. Perhaps the most important moment came on Christmas Day in 1927, when he signed a contract with CBS. His stay with CBS was long and prosperous. He was CBS's director of sports until July of 1946, after which he moved to WHN to work as a disc jockey—a move motivated by the higher salary offered by WHN.

Husing's contribution to the trade was immense. Unlike McNamee, who was always being shuffled around by NBC, Husing dived directly into sports. He hung around with the coaches and players at practice so that he would have detailed information for his broadcasts. Also, he hired as his assistant Les Quailey of CBS, who did such an outstanding job of research and preparation that almost anyone could have done well on the air.

Unfortunately, Quailey never received the accolades he deserved as Husing's "brains." Quailey was followed by Jimmy Dolan as Husing's assistant, and after Dolan came Walter Kennedy. These three men remained loyal to Husing through the years and each went on to bigger and better things.

Husing's contribution to broadcasting goes beyond his calling of games—he helped William S. Paley build CBS into the grand empire it became. Husing was Paley's office manager in 1928, and when Major Andrew White, who did most of the sports broadcasting for CBS at the time, was ill and couldn't make a trip to a Chicago football game, Husing suggested to Paley that he go as White's replacement. Husing was an instant success, and poor Major White never again received much airtime.

Husing's polished, aggressive broadcasting style did wonders for establishing CBS as a national powerhouse in the broadcast business. He was responsible for the growth and popularization of college bowl games by determining their locations and dates. The fact that the Orange Bowl and the Sugar Bowl are played on the same day and in the same place each year is the fruit of Husing's mania to compete directly with NBC and, more specifically, with McNamee.

Husing should be remembered for his greatest attribute—his desire to compete. Ultimately, however, it was this drive that led to the termination of his relationship with baseball. During the broadcast of the 1934 World Series, Husing, while on the air, openly criticized the umpires officiating at the event. As a result, Commissioner Landis, the "Second Most Powerful Man in America," outmuscled Paley at CBS, seeing to it that Husing never broadcast baseball again.

Jimmy Dolan (left) spots the action with binoculars as Ted Husing (right) calls the game for CBS. Before the advent of sophisticated technology, announcing events was usually too much for one man to handle.

Kenesaw Mountain Landis

To some, it may seem a bit much to say that Commissioner Landis had a defining role in radio broadcasting history. With a thorough understanding of his incredible control of the game (he denied integration and free agency), as well as of the media, however, any doubts concerning his importance to the development of this form will immediately be dispelled. After all, he was the most powerful man ever in Major League Baseball, and after his death safeguards were taken so that no one could ever dominate the sport in the same way. And after the novelty of the first announcers at games wore off, order had to be brought to what would become a multibillion-dollar industry.

When the Black Sox scandal broke in 1920, team owners needed a man to return order to baseball. Landis' familiarity with the game put him at the top of the owners' list.

A judge on the federal circuit in Chicago, Kenesaw Mountain Landis was elected Commissioner of Baseball on November 12, 1920, and was endowed with the power "to do anything I consider right in any matter detrimental to baseball." His initial contract was for seven years at fifty thousand dollars a year, active as of January 21, 1921. He remained Commissioner until his death at the age of seventy-eight on November 25, 1944. He was inducted into the Hall of Fame by special committee on December 9, 1944.

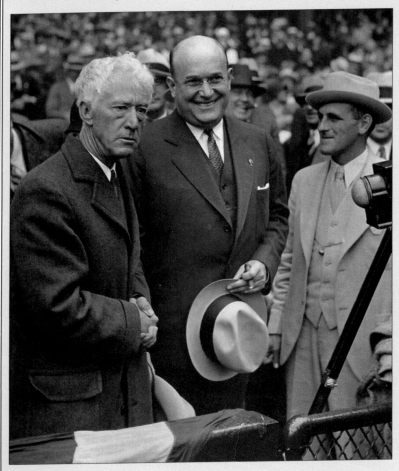

Commissioner Landis (left) at the opening game of the 1938 World Series at Yankee Stadium.

To a league caught in the margins, unable to secure its identity and on the verge of losing the trust of the public, Landis brought clarity and a frame of reference everyone understood. He has been described as conservative, intolerant, vindictive, bigoted, and shrewd. Opinions of his character vary, but it seems he had a clear vision of how to restore the image and prosperity of baseball. To the owners, Landis' credentials as a lawman showed that he was a man of inner conviction and an iron will. For example, in a 1907 rebate case that drew national attention, the judge had fined the colossal Standard Oil Company $29,240,000.

The name Kenesaw Mountain was given to him by his father, a Union soldier who lost his leg in 1864 in Cobb County, Georgia, where Kenesaw Mountain stands.

An excellent example of the power Landis had over the total baseball picture occurred at the 1935 World Series. Before a ball had even been pitched, Landis had determined how the game would be related to the public via radio. For the first time, NBC, CBS, and the brand new Mutual Broadcasting System would each have a team at the stadium to cover the action. The best announcers in the business were called upon to travel to the Series.

The trio of networks was on the cutting edge of national broadcasting, and since most of the country received all three networks, the competition was fierce. At 9:30 A.M. on the morning of the first game, Commissioner Landis called a meeting of the broadcast crews. As the men filed in, a polite "Good morning, Judge" was all that was heard. At nine-thirty sharp, the judge had the door closed and he went into his windup.

He began with a warm greeting addressed to Graham McNamee and then mentioned that one of the broadcasters of the past was absent, and that he need not go into that. He was referring to Ted Husing of CBS, who had second-guessed the umpires in a past Series broadcast. Landis had made

some phone calls after the Series and suggested to CBS that perhaps Husing wasn't the man for the Series. End of story: Husing never called another Series.

On this morning though, the Commissioner calmly smoked a cigarette and spelled out to the announcers how they, the best in the broadcast business, should conduct themselves. He told them to engage in simple reportage—to just report the action and not allow their opinions to become part of the broadcast. The umpires, the managers, and the two teams on the field were the best in their business, he said, and their actions should not be second-guessed, only reported.

This meeting had tremendous impact on all parties involved. The Commissioner, in his terrifying way, had set the rules for the industry. In one masterful stroke, he had defined a craft for some of the most influential voices the game has ever heard. Red Barber, for example, gained insight into his vocation from this meeting that would later enable him to overcome his self-admitted racism and call Jackie Robinson's name without flinching. Barber feels that his profession was legitimized by the credo that he was a radio journalist who detailed the events of America's game with an impartial and colorful eye. Emotion and partisanship were forsaken in favor of the cool head of a reporter.

There are some who have maintained that the game and its glory are defined by emotion—Mel Allen, with his "rooting" for the Yankees, is perhaps the best example of this school—but these men always had to keep a vigilant watch for the words that could have them removed from a broadcast.

Fans of baseball in 1920 looked on and were reassured that the integrity of the sport had been reasserted. The conservative judge and his position as czar of baseball stood as a testament to fair play and justice. Superficially, action had been taken by the owners, and the public, hungry for the excitement and energy of baseball, had nodded their approval.

Chicago

As it turned out, Chicago was the place to be if you were going to be any-body in radio baseball. The Windy City has spawned more broadcasters than any other locale, and their quality has been outstanding—of course, it goes without saying that there was no shortage of controversy either. In 1924, with the broadcasts of the October Classic and the All-Star game receiving much positive feedback, the move was made in Chicago to broadcast all regu-lar season home games by both the Cubs and the White Sox.

Hal Totten was the man to take the mike. Hailing from Illinois, the twenty-three-year-old Totten moved his desk from the rewrite room of the *Chicago Daily News* to station WMAQ, 670 AM. The station was owned by the *News* and the opportunity was one of a lifetime. Little did young Mr. Totten know that his success or failure would determine the fate of an industry. His performance was stable, his attitude humble, and his enthusiasm held in check, producing a season that was

Hal Totten in 1952, when he was the president of the Three I league in Class B baseball.

heard and loved by Chicago sports fans. Totten broadcast Cubs games for twenty-one years and during that time also covered the World Series twice for CBS with Major White. In the mid-1930s, NBC had him call the Series, and ultimately the Mutual Broadcast System had him calling their *Game of the Day* in the early 1950s.

Totten's signature signoff, "G'bye now," did not remain unchallenged for long. On April 14, 1925, Quin Ryan started calling games over station WGN. On one memorable occasion, Ryan chronicled Grover Cleveland pitching an 8–2 victory and hitting a single, a double, and a home run.

Because there were no laws established to secure the exclusive

Quin Ryan, shown here around 1940, pioneered the broadcasting of professional baseball games in Chicago in 1925.

rights to a game in the 1920s, whoever could get equipment into Wrigley Field or Comiskey Park was free to broadcast. William Wrigley, the Cubs' hallowed owner and a man of great wisdom, was extremely fond of radio broadcasts of his club's games. "The more outlets the better," he said with the intent of clogging the city with news of his team's exploits. Through the 1920s, as many as seven stations were bringing Chicago's baseball games to the public. For the most part, only five—three carrying the Cubs and two the White Sox—were successful.

Pat Flanagan on WBBM called both Cubs and White Sox games. He broadcast three World Series for CBS before retiring in 1943. Charlie "Jolly Cholly" Grimm, first baseman for the Cubs from 1925 to 1936, would later become a boothmate of Flanagan's in the late thirties and early forties. Grimm also managed the Cubs at three different times, exposing the close relationship maintained between management and broadcasters. In 1960, for example, Lou Boudreau replaced Grimm as manager, and the following year Grimm left the booth and became one of the original members of the Cubs' College of Coaches, with Boudreau moving to the announcer's booth. The bottom line was that sponsors paid the broadcaster and therefore had say over who was on the air, but the public wanted an educated announcer, and all recognized, even early on, that an educated announcer was the best

The Hoosier Hot Shots

A novelty band of the Depression era, the Hoosier Hot Shots featured hick clothes, a vaudeville style, and cornball appeal. They gained national recognition in 1935 via the widely popular *National Barn Dance*, which was broadcast over WLS Chicago on Saturday nights. The thirties were a decade of extremes in the United States, and perhaps the Hot Shots' success is partly linked to that trend. The "Gas House Gang," the St. Louis Cardinals' famous cut-ups, entertained baseball fans throughout the country with their vaudevillian antics. The Hoosier Hot Shots seem also to have struck a certain chord in America's heart. At the height of their popularity, they were in the studios often and were also appearing frequently in low-budget westerns. Their version of "Take Me Out to the Ball Game" brings a smile to the faces of all who hear it.

Above: In 1935, Cubs manager and first baseman Charlie Grimm engineered a spectacular twenty-one-game winning streak at the end of the season to win the pennant. Below: Cubs owner William Wrigley.

announcer. During the early twenties, personalities that could be heard over the radio waves included comedian Joe E. Brown; Quin Ryan, WGN program manager; Truman Bradley, later of television *Science Fiction Theater* fame; Johnny O'Hara; John Harrington; Jack Drees, of horse racing announcing fame; Russ Hodges, the voice of the New York and San Francisco Giants from 1949 to 1970; and Bob Elson, who would call games for thirty-eight years.

As was implied earlier, much of the credit for the wild growth of radio broadcasting in Chicago must be given to William Wrigley and his vision of radio as a promotional tool for the popularization of his club. He was the first to have a "Ladies' Day" promoted over the radio, thereby tapping a huge audience—women—that had been neglected for too long. Wrigley also had the first glass-partitioned announcer's booth installed in the stadium.

The Dial Expands

After Chicago's broadcasts of Cubs games proved successful, other cities soon followed suit, airing home games played by their local teams. From Philadelphia's Shibe Park and Baker Bowl, respectively, Athletics and Phillies

fans could hear Bill Dyer call their favorite teams' games. In 1927, Garnett Marks could be heard calling games from Sportsman's Park in St. Louis. Two years later, France Laux moved from KVOO Tulsa to 50,000-watt KMOX, replacing Marks as the principal announcer for the Cardinals and the Browns. Laux remained in St. Louis until 1953, when Anheuser-Busch Brewery bought the Cards and the Browns moved to Baltimore. For eighteen years, Laux was heard over KMOX as the voice of St. Louis baseball. He broadcast the World Series for CBS from 1933 through 1938.

Because Laux chronicled so many great aspects of baseball, it is hard to pick a short list. He spoke daily of Marty Marion's utility and range as a fielder, as well as the Dean brothers' command of the pitching mound—in 1934 they had a combined record of 49–18)—and was at the mike for the first night game the Browns played, an event that was actually more of a party than a game. In 1945, he called one-armed pitcher Pete Gray's debut against the Tigers. At the All-Star game in 1934, he called Carl Hubbell's herculean feat of striking out five future Hall of Fame batters successively. (Using his screwball, Hubbell had

France Laux saw more high jinks perpetrated on the diamond —in the form of the antics of the "Gas House Gang"—than any other announcer.

fanned Ruth, Gehrig, and Jamie Foxx to end the first inning, and then wiffed Al Simmons and Joe Cronin to start the second.)

In 1925, stations WAAB and WNAC, an affiliate of the Colonial Network and later the Yankee Networks in New England (from Augusta, Maine, to Hartford, Connecticut), had former sportswriter Fred Hoey spinning the tales of the hapless Red Sox and Braves. Hoey was extremely popular; he

soon became a household name. In 1931, there was a "Fred Hoey Day" at the ballpark, at which he was presented with a three-thousand-dollar check and a scroll, and then made a speech about his love of the community. He was an idol for many of the Boston-area youngsters who wanted to become broadcasters. He pioneered collegiate and professional ice hockey games on radio and was responsible for turning Boston fans into (arguably) the most fanatical in the nation.

Southpaw Carl Hubbell depended on his screwball to baffle batters, and gained immortality in the second All-Star game (1935) by fanning five legends.

Hoey's story reveals a great deal about the spirit of the times and the personalities involved in early radio broadcasting. Born in the Boston suburb of Saxonville, Hoey grew up to be a lonely man who had a drinking problem. At the moment of his greatest success as a broadcaster, the 1933 World Series, Hoey had to be pulled from the mike in the second or third inning because of a "bad cold." In reality, Hoey's "bad cold" was excessive drunkenness. Amazingly enough, the Boston fans threw their support to Hoey, writing thousands of letters in his defense and chastising those responsible for pulling him from the game.

Hoey was replaced in 1937—at the height of his fame—by Frankie Frisch, when General Mills, sponsor for the games at that time, decided that Hoey and his coarse, barking style had to go. When this news reached the fans, protests were immediately heard. The newspapers, the radio stations, and General Mills were inundated with letters from fans appealing for Hoey's reinstatement. The story became front-page copy, and a boycott by the fans was independently organized. Both the Braves and the Red Sox ballparks were picketed by angry fans. This is more than remarkable—it is frightening. The protest (which some say was more like a riot) was so effective that Hoey was returned to the mike. Two years later, in 1939, Cliff Samuelson of General Mills again had Hoey replaced (this time successfully) by Frisch.

Although Hoey's style was unpolished, no one from Boston ever uttered a word against him. Even with the Yankee Networks' policy of going to news at six o'clock sharp, regardless of the score, inning, or situation, Hoey's emotional broadcasts flourished until 1939.

Baseball's Geography

Although baseball was popular throughout the United States, it was in the Northeast that professional baseball got its start. Financial backing for new ball clubs came mostly from eastern bankers and industrialists, and because it was understood that teams located near concentrated populations that could use mass transit to get to games would have the greatest chance for success, most teams were based in large cities.

In 1920, the National and American leagues were in place, but not as we know them today. The National League teams were, in order of finishing, the Brooklyn Dodgers, the New York Giants, the Cincinnati Reds, the Pittsburgh Pirates, the Chicago Cubs, the St. Louis Cardinals, the Boston Braves (who were called the Boston Bees from 1936 to 1941), and the Philadelphia Phillies. The American League consisted of the Cleveland Indians, the Chicago White Sox, the New York Yankees, the St. Louis Browns, the Boston Red Sox, the Washington Senators, the Detroit Tigers, and the Philadelphia Athletics.

The expansion of the majors took place in stages. In 1953, the Boston Braves moved to Milwaukee; in 1954, the St. Louis Browns moved to Baltimore; and in 1955, the A's moved to Kansas City. In 1958, the Brooklyn Dodgers moved to Los Angeles and the New York Giants to San Francisco. In 1961, the A.L. expanded to ten teams, with the Washington Senators becoming the Minnesota Twins and new franchises being awarded to Washington (again called the Senators) and Los Angeles (the Angels).

The Mets and Astros joined the N.L. in 1962, and in 1967, Atlanta joined the N.L. when the Braves moved there from Milwaukee. In 1968, the A's moved from Kansas City to Oakland. The year 1969

Cincinnati's Crosley Field during the 1939 World Series. Note that there are lights at the stadium.

Despite the Depression, baseball was immensely popular in Chicago, in part because of aggressive promotion of the sport via radio. The Cubs won three pennants in the thirties, but their last Series victory was in 1908.

saw both leagues expand to twelve teams, as the A.L. added the Kansas City Royals and the Seattle Pilots, while the N.L. added the San Diego Padres and the Montreal Expos. In 1970, the Pilots moved to Milwaukee, changing their name to the Brewers. In 1972, the Texas Rangers debuted—they were, in fact, the transplanted Washington Senators and had entered the A.L. in 1961. In 1977, the American League again underwent expansion, adding the Seattle Mariners and the Toronto Blue Jays. And most recently, in 1993, the N.L. again expanded, adding to its roster of teams the Florida Marlins and the Colorado Rockies.

Boston's Fenway Park remains one of the three "classic" parks of the major leagues—the other two are Wrigley Field and Tiger Stadium.

Hoey died of asphyxiation on November 17, 1949—his body was discovered by a delivery boy in a gas-filled kitchen. This was a tragic loss; Fred Hoey was one of the best-loved voices of baseball.

Frankie Frisch, known as the "Fordham Flash," had been an outstanding infielder for both the Giants and the Cards. As player-manager for the Cards for five years (1933 through 1937), he knew great success leading the "Gas House Gang" to a World Series victory in 1934. His Boston assignment (replacing Hoey) was his first as an announcer, and it did not go very smoothly; winning over the tough Boston fans, who were predisposed to dislike him because he was an outsider, was no picnic. Frequently, he would lie in bed at night in his hotel room and hear picketers marching and hollering in the street. Luckily, he left after a year to manage the Pirates, but he returned to the booth at the Polo Grounds for two years before ending up as the Cubs' manager.

In Cleveland, a young man named Tom Manning began calling plays for the Indians in the mid-twenties. Manning's "training" in broadcasting dated back to his boyhood, when he was dubbed "the paperboy with the loudest voice." On the urging of someone within the Indians organization, Manning became a fixture in the park, calling games through a megaphone. Eventually, he was set up behind the batter's box with a primitive amplifier. Later, an executive at WTAM heard him in the park and decided that he should call games over the radio. Manning debuted in 1925, but appeared only intermittently at this time; he was made a regular announcer in 1928.

Manning was responsible for introducing many Indians fans to radio. His style was pure entertainment: humorous and energetic. The town was on holiday when Manning was at the mike.

In 1931, the Indians' flagship station switched from WTAM to WHK, and Jack Graney, the first player-turned-announcer, took over the reins for the Tribe's broadcasts. Later (1948 to 1967), Jimmy Dudley joined Graney in the booth, eventually replacing Graney as the voice of the Indians.

Frankie Frisch, the "Fordham Flash," finishes his fluid swing. In his day, the telephoto lens had not yet been invented, and sports photographers were forced to stand along the edges of the diamond to get their shots.

Left to right: Hank Greenberg, first base; Leon "Goose" Goslin, outfield; Charlie Gehringer, second base; and Ervin "Pete" Fox, right field, of the 1935 Detroit Tigers.

An alcoholic, Manning had trouble with the day-to-day routine of being a staff broadcaster; as a result, WTAM took him off the air in 1932. Despite this, NBC executives hired him as a part-timer, because of his great popularity, and through 1955, Manning broadcast three heavyweight title fights and nine World Series, many with McNamee, Hal Totten, and Red Barber.

The city of Detroit was another community where baseball was the main event. The tough working-class population took its Tigers seriously; they drank hard and cheered harder. This was not a place for the weak of heart or those who lacked conviction. Enter Ty Tyson on April 19, 1927, the year after Ty Cobb left Detroit for the Philadelphia A's. From Navin Field, this native of Tyrone, Pennsylvania, called his first game over WWJ. Tyson was a sensation in the baseball-hungry region. He had a slow, staccato delivery that he used to make Goose Goslin, catcher-manager Mickey Cochrane (known as "Black Mike"), and Charlie Gehringer (the "Mechanical Man") come alive for the WWJ listening area.

It was a magical era for the Tigers, as they bounced from the cellar in the late twenties to the pennant in 1934 and 1935, with Ty calling the games all the way. Station WWJ did not have a sponsor backing the broadcast until 1934. Before that, radio coverage was a "public service."

Cardinals infielder Pepper Martin stands up at third base during the 1934 All-Star game.

At this time, the Gillette Company and the Commissioner of Baseball were responsible for selecting the announcers for the World Series and All-Star game broadcasts. In 1934, when the Tigers went all the way to the Series, Commissioner Landis named the network trios: Ted Husing, Pat Flanagan, and France Laux would broadcast for CBS, and Graham McNamee, Tom Manning, and Ford Bond would call games on NBC. The exclusion of Tyson, the local favorite, the Commissioner reported, was based on his "excessive partisanship."

Outraged and mobilized, the people of Michigan flooded the Commissioner's office with a staggering six-hundred-thousand-signature petition that forced the judge to reconsider his decision. The final verdict allowed Tyson to broadcast locally over WWJ, and Tiger fans heard Tyson tell of the Gas House Gang defeating the Tigers in seven games. The following year, Tyson was given a seat on the NBC network to call the Series, and the Tigers were victorious over the Cubs four games to two.

In Cincinnati in 1929, Bob Burdette began airing Reds games from the rooftop of Crosley Field. He did not last long, however. In February of 1930, Harry Hartman cajoled Sid Weil, the owner of the Reds, into making a change in the broadcast booth. Hartman's logic was simple: The club needed a more exciting voice. Burdette was moved to station WLW while Hartman occupied the WFBE booth. For four years, the five-foot-six, 320-pound Hartman doubled as the radio broadcaster of choice and public address announcer at the stadium. His mike-juggling act was second nature to him, and he proved to be a great entertainer for the Cincinnati faithful.

His sponsors—Black Peter cigarettes, Frank's Radio Shop, and patent medicine Udga—were part of Harry's daily ritual (he actually used the products, and frequented the store, that he endorsed). Spectators at renamed Redland Field adored Hartman's grassroots style. He was uneducated and a bit rough around the edges, very much like Cincinnati at the time. He favored expressions such as *sacko, whammo, belto,* and *bammo* to describe the action on the field.

The 1930s: The Make-or-Break Decade

In the early thirties, radio and baseball grew both together and apart. Some baseball bigwigs, such as William Wrigley and Larry McPhail, then acting president of the Cincinnati Reds, endorsed radio as a tool to promote their teams. Others, such as the New York team owners, felt that radio would undercut their revenues at the gate. The only means of generating revenue was through ticket sales; there was very little merchandising at the time, and what little there was, was not selling to the populace, for they were too busy combating the Depression.

Even in cities that had two teams, such as Chicago, St. Louis, Philadelphia, and Boston, there was a strict agreement that only the team playing at home would be aired. It was not a technical problem, but rather convention—the team playing at home would receive preferential treatment from the network or local station. In the case of a rainout, or if no home game were scheduled, stations would broadcast a game locally from an away team's park. This policy remained until the mid-1940s (after World War II), when all games of all teams began to be broadcast.

The rationale behind the 1930s policy to air only home games was that radio was still merely an advertisement for the game. Because the owners did not yet truly understand the significance of the broadcasts—that is, what effect they had on attendance

Larry McPhail was not only a powerful baseball executive, but also a staunch supporter of radio as a promotional tool.

Who Runs Baseball?

The baseball industry is structured very much like feudal Europe. The owners are independent lords who have banded together in order to secure their power and provide security for all under their dominion. They regulate themselves and, oddly enough, are exempt from the laws adopted in the United States to break monopolies and illegal trusts. The owners' contention is that baseball's success through the decades has resulted in purity of control and lack of governmental interference.

Before "free agency," there existed a clear division of labor between management and players that allowed for owners to monopolize the athletes' services through a "reserve clause." This clause was the evolution of an agreement made in 1879 to keep players' salaries under the control of management. In short, the "reserve clause" made players the property of a single club, and unless the player was traded or the team relinquished its rights to him, the player was bound exclusively to that club. This relationship defied the antitrust laws

Commissioner Landis (seated, at center) and presidents of the major league franchises at their annual December meeting in 1934.

that had been installed to reform large corporations in the United States.

In 1915, the Federal League, headed by coal magnate James A. Gilmore, failed in its attempt to compete with the two established leagues. A lawsuit was brought (Judge Landis presided) and a settlement ensued. Some players in the Federal League were picked up by A.L. and N.L. teams, and owners in the Federal League received monetary compensation for their damages.

The Baltimore franchise, however, did not share in the settlement for losses incurred by the Federal League's dissolution, and it brought a suit against organized baseball

that ultimately went to the Supreme Court. Chief Justice Oliver Wendell Holmes, well-known for his liberal decisions, ruled in 1922 that the sport of baseball was not "interstate commerce" and therefore was immune to the liability the Baltimore franchise was claiming. This arrangement provided the owners with security and the players with no bargaining power at the negotiating table. The exploitation of the players was thus secured by the nation's highest judicial body.

Since the owners had complete control over their marketplace, the nucleus of the league, located in the Northeast, took root securely. Although this ensured the success and close familiarity of the players, teams, and fans, it exempted the league from laws that had been established to protect workers from unfair labor practices and provide them a voice in their trade.

Baseball's Commissioner is an even higher power than the owners. Of course, the owners are usually in sympathy with the Commissioner, but there were, and still are, times when the two did not agree. For example, Landis outlawed gentlemen's agreements and cover-ups of player transactions, such as optioning players to the minors without proper paperwork. This forced owners to be up-front with players as well as with other teams interested in the acquisition of players by virtue of their status in the league.

Landis was always quick to act, and had a clear philosophy concerning baseball: It would take his image. Anyone who defied him would come out on the losing end. For example, on October 16, 1921, he banned World Series participants from playing in postseason barnstorming tours. Babe Ruth, Bob Meusel, and pitcher Bill Piercy defied his edict, and Ruth openly challenged the Commissioner. Landis responded by fining the players the amount of their World Series bonus—$3,362.26—and suspending them until May 20 of the ensuing season. Even Babe Ruth was not above the control of the Commissioner's office.

and the support of the fans—they felt that if away games were aired, fans simply would not attend the games being played at home, and revenues would drop. Radio broadcasting, however, was not merely advertising; it was a tool that contributed directly to the popularization of the sport and, when used properly, of a particular club by increasing the audience beyond the confines of the park.

Some owners went further than limiting broadcasts only to home games—in 1932, all three New York franchises agreed that no games would be broadcast in any form, live or re-created. The New York owners, unlike the forward-thinking owners of Chicago and Philadelphia clubs, felt that radio was hurting the game as well as their pocketbooks. Their ban lasted until 1939, when Larry McPhail became owner of the Brooklyn Dodgers and brought Red Barber with him from Cincinnati. McPhail's defiance of the moratorium on radio broadcasts forced the Giants and Yankees to broadcast in order to compete for fans' attention.

Yankee Stadium in 1938. That year marked the last Series broadcast over three competing networks—NBC, CBS, and Mutual. In 1939, Gillette bought the exclusive rights and limited the broadcast to one network.

When it came to re-creations, there was great controversy over how games should be presented—as fanciful "shows," complete with sound effects, or in the form of simple reportage.

Re-creations and a Rift in the Business

It was at this time that re-creations, via Western Union's monopoly of telegraph lines, became the backbone of the radio baseball industry. Because broadcasters did not travel with teams and thus could not call away games, most baseball games heard at the time were re-created in studios. Also, networks expanded at this time with the aim of opening new markets, which always demanded baseball.

Newspaper reporters had been using Western Union's lines to send updates of their stories to their offices so that printing could commence as soon as the action finished. Following the reporters' lead, radio broadcasters adopted the supplemental "Paragraph One" briefs of each inning so that they could work their own magic with the details in the studio.

A schism in the broadcast field soon developed between those who regarded the re-creations as theater and those who considered themselves journalists. The thespians went to great lengths, adding crowd noise complete with young men selling ice cream, to stock "soundtracks" of umpires calling the pitches accompanied by the chatter of players encouraging each other on the field and from the dugout. The journalistic school felt this duplicity misinformed the audience and distorted the primary function of the broadcaster, which was to call the game. The entertainment dimension of the program should be based upon the announcer's ability to engage an audience without conning the fans into thinking they were at the game. If an announcer were truly a professional, the audience should appreciate hearing the telegraph noise coupled with the commentary of the broadcaster.

Re-creations

Ted Husing (left), vice president Dawes (center), and sending operator Harry Schneider (right) demonstrate the telegraph.

The first intercity telegraph line in the United States was in place by 1844. The technology had existed since 1837, when Samuel Morse, Alfred Vail, and Joseph Henry had collaborated on the development and patent of a telegraph system.

Following the lead of the writers at the ballpark, radio broadcasters adopted the use of Western Union's telegraph lines. There were no restrictions prohibiting broadcasting, so if you had a transmitter and the money to pay Western Union, you were in business. Some reasonably notable personalities gained entrance into showbiz doing re-creations, among them Ronald "Dutch" Reagan, who broadcast Cubs and White Sox games over WHO, Des Moines, Iowa, through the mid-1930s.

A radio station would have two people at the stadium, one to watch and dictate the events in shorthand format, and another skilled in Morse code to send messages. At the other end of the cable would be a technician who would decipher the transmission and a radio personality who would "re-create" the events at the ballpark in a variety of ways. The task was at times confusing, because of the codes: SWS meant "strike one swinging" and B2W stood for "ball 2 wide." The rest of the "action" was left to the imagination of the announcer.

Some announcers were purists who allowed the listening audience to hear the telegraph, doing little to conceal the fact that the game was a re-creation, while others went to elaborate lengths to animate the transmission. Arch McDonald, "The Old Pine Tree" or "The Rembrandt of the Re-Creation," did everything possible to make games played by the hapless Washington Senators more exciting. For a time, McDonald staged his re-creations from the second floor of the People's Drugstore on G Street, about three blocks from the White House. In the heat of the D.C. summer, McDonald would shed his clothes and broadcast in his underwear, and people would stop on the sidewalk in front of the store and watch him. Later, a studio was installed in the basement of the building with bleacher seats lining the walls so the public could come and take part in the broadcast. McDonald and Western Union operators would be in the middle of the room unfolding the hottest ticket in town.

Rosey Rowswell's act for the Pirates (1936 to 1954) featured his signature line, "Get upstairs, Aunt Minnie, and raise the window!," whenever one of the Bucs hit a home run. Moments after this line was spoken, assistant Bob Prince would shatter panes of glass and drop a tray laden with bells and metal objects to create a clamor in response to Aunt Minnie's predicament. With Ralph Kiner batting for the Pirates from 1946 to 1954—he hit fifty-one home runs in 1947 and fifty-four in 1949—Rowswell and Prince went through a lot of glass.

Doing re-creations was a touch-and-go proposition. Cable lines were frequently severed, leaving the broadcaster in the studio with no information and no inkling as to when the problem would be solved and the transmission restored. When this happened, some opted to play music or variety programming with the promise of returning to the game as soon as possible. Others took a

more duplicitous tack, having the last man at the plate indefinitely fouling off pitches.

The height of re-creations was not until the late forties, however, when Gordon McLendon, "The Old Scotchman," established the Liberty Broadcasting System, with the Liberty Baseball Network its core. Liberty exploited the baseball law prohibiting the broadcast of any game within seventy-five miles of the ballpark by a station not in the established networks.

McLendon, whose flagship station was KLIF Dallas, did not need to worry about competition. The Western market, with its population of between 60 and 90 million people, was wide open. Rather than sticking to only one team, Liberty's *Game of the Day* and *Game of the Night* featured the best game being played. McLendon's impact and profit were tremendous, but in 1952 he brought suit against Major League Baseball, claiming that their laws were "illegally hindering and restricting a free and natural flow of commerce." This episode backfired, and baseball's governing body retaliated by pulling the plug on Liberty's access to Western Union lines; by 1952, Liberty was bankrupt.

Ronald "Dutch" Reagan announcing a game in the mid-thirties.

Sponsors and the Rise of Modern Broadcasting

In September of 1934, Commissioner Landis sold the World Series broadcast rights to the Ford Motor Company for four years at $100,000 a year. Never before had a sponsor had to pay for, or even had the opportunity to purchase, exclusive rights to the Series broadcast.

The year 1934 offered baseball fans both fond farewells and warm welcomes. Babe Ruth announced his last season, but added that he wanted to manage and pinch-hit. Joe DiMaggio was traded from the San Francisco team of the Pacific Coast League to the Yankees organization.

In 1933, Sid Weil had lost ownership of the Cincinnati Reds, and the bank had brought in Larry McPhail. The new administrator immediately sold controlling interest of the team to Powel Crosley, who owned radio stations WLW and WSAI. These two stations were technologically more powerful than Harry Hartman's WFBE and therefore stood as a valuable and important ally for the slumping Reds. McPhail, a student of Branch Rickey, was kept on to clean up the Reds organization and in so doing allowed only twenty home games to be aired in 1934. The following year, 1935, after realizing that radio encouraged fans to attend games rather than keeping them from the parks, McPhail threw his full weight behind radio.

Debuting in Cincinnati in 1934 over station WSAI was Red Barber. Then only twenty-six years old, Barber made the pathetic Reds come to life as no one had ever done before. The popular Harry Hartman soon became second fiddle to the Ol' Redhead's sermons from the park. At the time, three different, and competing, voices could be heard announcing Reds games: Barber on WSAI, Hartman on WFBE, and "Oatmeal" Brown on WKRC.

Joe DiMaggio had to hit safely in forty-five games to break Wee Willie Keeler's 1897 record.

In December of 1934, the National League voted to permit seven night games for any team that installed lights in its stadium. The American League did not grant permission for night games until 1937.

The Babe

So much has been written about George Herman "Babe" Ruth that he should be considered one of the most important people of the twentieth century. Despite this, little is known about the Babe's moments on the radio. For example, "The Babe Ruth Home Run Story," a song of 1920, was the first song recorded to honor a baseball player.

Also, the Babe had his own radio program in the 1940s, called *Here's Babe Ruth*, which ran on NBC. The version of "Take Me Out to the Ball Game" (first recorded in 1908 by the Hayden Quartet and/or Edward Meeker) that served as the program's theme song was sung by 350 children in the studio, and their enthusiasm fired up the Babe for his radio show, which featured many of baseball's top names of the day. Kids would ask questions of Ruth and his guest as well as learn about the rationing of supplies for the war effort through commercial spots by sponsors such as Spalding.

An interesting footnote in Ruth's baseball career concerns an early radio experience. As the story goes, Ruth accepted an invitation from Harold Arlin in Pittsburgh to do a radio interview. The going wasn't always smooth in the pioneering days of 1921, and Arlin, planning ahead for any possible snags—live radio is, of course, subject to many contingencies—scripted the interview for Babe.

Upon arrival at the William Penn Hotel, Ruth received his script and Arlin began his show by introducing Babe and asking the first question. Babe froze, rendered dumb. Arlin grabbed the lines from Ruth and assumed both roles. Ruth, attempting to regain his composure, leaned against a wall, smoking a cigarette and presumably enjoying "his" interview. Ironically, people wrote letters to KDKA and commented on the beauty of the timbre of the Babe's resonant voice.

Although their relationship started on slightly duplicitous grounds, the Babe and radio soon came to feed off each other. The Bambino's career promoted radio, and radio, in turn, promoted the Babe.

One of the most moving moments in baseball history is Ruth's farewell from Yankee Stadium in 1948. It was June 13, and the occasion marked the retiring of Ruth's number, 3, as well as the twenty-fifth anniversary of the "House that Ruth Built." Babe died of throat cancer on August 16, 1948, and on his last day at the stadium his raspy, fragile voice filled all who heard it with the pain of a legend who would die at the age of fifty-three.

Red Barber

As a consequence of the other teams not being able to find a sponsor, Barber was the only announcer calling games in New York in 1943. He succeeded Ted Husing as director of sports at CBS in July of 1946. He called Army-Navy games, professional football championships, five All-Star games, thirteen World Series, and many Rose, Orange, and Sugar bowls. He finally moved to syndicated radio after the Yankees fired him.

In 1953, Barber, who was scheduled to broadcast the Series with Mel Allen, asked to negotiate his own contract with Gillette rather than follow standard procedure. The "standard procedure" was to graciously accept whatever Gillette paid, which was outrageously low for the most important broadcast in the industry. Barber, a veteran announcer and perhaps the most respected man in his trade, felt he deserved more money. Gillette told Red he could take it or leave it, and Barber left it. He was the only man ever to turn down a Series job on principle.

Walter "Red" Barber was born in Columbus, Mississippi, on February 17, 1908. He reluctantly entered the radio business while at the University of Florida—by reading over the radio a paper on bovine obstetrics in exchange for a meal!

While many broadcasters of the era were content simply to entertain, Barber actually studied the game, emphasizing statistics, tendencies, and rituals of players. He did this in order to relate the game in toto—humanizing players as people who had families, likes, and dislikes just as the fans did.

Barber broadcast for the Reds from 1934 to 1938, for the Brooklyn Dodgers from 1939 to 1953, and finally, for the Yankees from 1954 to 1966. Barber's career is the handrail that provides the path through the modern broadcasting era.

During World War II, he used his microphone and immense popularity to organize blood donations for Red Cross drives and to initiate the War Bond Radio Telephone Sale, which raised legal tender for the war effort and increased consciousness of the situation overseas and at home.

This episode serves to illustrate Barber's character. In 1947, he handled the integration issue with his typical aplomb—although he later admitted that he did not find it easy to call Robinson's name—perhaps contributing to the ultimate pacification of those angered by the move. After a serious illness in 1948, Barber turned deeply religious and his famous baseball sermons became less metaphorical.

His book *The Broadcasters* and his contributions to radio offer the most distinguished career the profession has ever known. His boothmates in Brooklyn, Connie Desmond and Vin Scully (his proud protégé and the man some consider the best in the business today), were profoundly affected by the beauty and eloquence Barber brought to baseball coverage. On August 7, 1978, Red Barber and Mel Allen became the first announcers inducted into the Hall of Fame.

Above: One hundred sixteen 1,500-watt lamps lit Crosley Field at the first night game. Below: Arch McDonald brought the hapless Washington Senators to life on the radio.

The brand-new Mutual Broadcasting Network was formed in the summer of 1935 and debuted on May 24 with the first night game played in the major leagues: the Cincinnati Reds hosting the Philadelphia Phillies. Red Barber was the announcer as the Reds won 2–1. As a promotional stunt, McPhail coaxed President Franklin D. Roosevelt to flip a ceremonial switch from the White House lighting the park.

On air in the nation's capital in 1934 was "The Old Pine Tree," Arch McDonald. He announced Senators (or "Nats") games from Griffith Stadium for twenty-two years, gaining stature as one of the most entertaining and proficient re-creation experts in the game. The flamboyant McDonald arrived in Washington the year after the Nats won the pennant, but instead of inheriting a glorious franchise, he ended up calling games for a decidedly depressed ballclub.

Heard over station WJSV (later WTOP), McDonald coined such phrases as "ducks on the pond," meaning runners on base, and "right down Broadway," which referred to a pitch thrown over the middle of the plate. He even had a gong in the studio on which he would pound out the number of bases a hit earned. McDonald began his career in Chattanooga doing re-creations for baseball's showman of showmen, Joe Engel. A southerner through and through, McDonald had the typical southern drawl and slowness of speech, which led to his appellation "the Master of the Pause." His more popular moniker, "The Old Pine Tree," came from the hillbilly song "They Cut Down the Old Pine Tree," which he used to break into when the Nats stopped an opposing team's rally.

In 1939, McDonald moved to New York to call Yankee games. McDonald was the man who dubbed Joe DiMaggio the "Yankee Clipper." His stint in the Big Apple lasted only a year, but he made quite an impact on the cosmopolitan city with his down-home appeal.

McDonald, a staunch Democrat who ran for Congress in 1944 from Montgomery County, Maryland, was also something of a politico. His longtime friend Happy Chandler, a U.S. Senator, became Commissioner of Baseball in 1946 and gave McDonald a seat on the Series broadcast that year.

McDonald's performance at the 1946 Series was less than electrifying. As the story goes, there was a lot of silence during the broadcast and many wanted McDonald removed from the mike. Chandler went to the broadcaster's booth to talk to "The Old Pine Tree," and when he returned, he informed everyone that he had in fact touched McDonald to see if he was warm and breathing—happily, he was both—and as long as the announcer remained in that condition he would continue to broadcast the games.

In 1934, the legendary Detroit slugger Harry Heilmann (who was inducted into the Hall of Fame on July 21, 1952) began broadcasting Tigers games over the Michigan Radio Network, owned by George W. Trendle, creator of such radio programs as *The Lone Ranger* and *Call of the Yukon*. The Tigers Network was two-pronged, with Heilmann broadcasting over flagship station WXYZ to outlying regions of Michigan while Tyson broadcast locally over WWJ to the Detroit metropolitan area. As a result, Heilmann entered into indirect competition with Ty Tyson.

Heilmann's first few years were rough while he slowly learned his trade, but he lasted for seventeen years, until 1950. With his down-home

Slugger Harry Heilmann became a popular announcer when he moved from field to booth because fans appreciated his first-hand experience and outlook on the game.

vernacular that didn't strive for the stars but rather was comfortable with the familiar, the "Old Slug," as he was known to some, gained a following to rival that of Barber, McNamee, Tyson, and Allen.

The 1935 Series was a significant moment in radio broadcast history. It was the first year without McNamee on the air and the first year with Red Barber. Before the Series, Mutual was operating with three stations: WOR in New York, WGN in Chicago, and CKLW in Detroit. As fate would have it, Commissioner Landis said he would recognize Mutual as a network and allow it to broadcast the Series if it admitted station WLW Cincinnati, which had previously been affiliated with NBC. WLW station manager John Clark agreed to Landis' proposal with the stipulation that his young announcer Red Barber be a part of the Series broadcast. Landis agreed, and Mutual had as its broadcast team Barber, Bob Elson, and Quin Ryan, the "old-timer," as the color man (both Elson and Ryan were from Chicago). The Tigers defeated the Cubs in six games to become the world champions.

In 1936 Barber debuted in the New York area, calling the Series for NBC with Tom Manning and Ty Tyson; the Series was again held at the Polo Grounds, and the Giants lost to the Yankees in six games. In that same year, thirteen teams in the major leagues regularly broadcast games.

Rosey Rowswell and "Aunt Millie." Rowswell was an American treasure—his broadcasts were ironic, slapstick, and profound.

From Forbes Field in Pittsburgh came the fanatical Bucs fan, poet, humorist, author, and broadcast legend, Albert Kennedy (Rosey) Rowswell. Rowswell's calls of the bases being "FOB"—full of Bucs—and "doozie marooney"—an extra base hit—brought excitement to the city from 1936 to 1954.

In the matter of re-creations, Rowswell was most certainly not a purist, and his embellished broadcasts were an attempt to enhance baseball's popularity through theatrics. Those who tuned in to him became hooked not only on the Bucs, but on Rosey's story-telling. This aspect of Rowswell's style serves to illustrate that his legacy was founded on emotion and inspiration. He never attempted to be an impartial reporter of the action, but instead rooted vigorously for his beloved Bucs. The fans of the Pirates understood his passion, and their loyalty and love for Rowswell inspired such future broadcasters as Bob Prince, Harry Caray, and Bert Wilson.

The year 1939 introduced many new wrinkles to the mature face of baseball. On June 12, the dedication of the Baseball Hall of Fame Museum

Sam and Dave

O ne of the definitive soul bands of the sixties and seventies, Sam and Dave first performed together in 1961 at Miami's King of Hearts club. Both hailed from southern climes, Sam Moore from Miami and David Prater from Ocilla, Georgia.

Sam and Dave's urgent appeal had its roots in gospel music. Their break in the music business came in the mid-sixties when Jerry Wexler had them sign with Atlantic Records and teamed them with the staff writing team of Isaac Hayes and David Porter. Their hits included "You Don't Know Like I Know" (1966), "Soul Man" (1967), and "Soul Sister, Brown Sugar" (1969). Unfortunately, due to personal differences the duo split in 1970; Dave Prater died in 1988.

"Knock It Out of the Park" is a fitting tribute to baseball from two men who undoubtedly knew that the game is ruled by passion.

The Hall of Fame dedication in 1939 was the greatest assembly of baseball talent ever.

was held at Doubleday Field in Cooperstown, New York. This event was the greatest assembly of baseball legends ever; among those in attendance were Ty Cobb, Honus Wagner, Cy Young, Babe Ruth, Walter Johnson, Connie Mack, Commissioner Landis, and Nap Lajoie. The dedication's finale was a six-inning all-star game featuring all players in attendance. The affair was broadcast by Tom Manning.

Also in 1939, the Red Sox showed off rookie Ted Williams, Lou Gehrig retired, Larry McPhail was elected president of the Dodgers, and on August 26, NBC's W2XBS broadcast the first baseball game on television—the Reds at Brooklyn's Ebbets Field, with Barber at the mike. The night before, the American League had played its first night game at Shribe Park, with Cleveland beating the A's 8–3 in ten innings.

The thirties were the make-or-break era for broadcast baseball. Many in America were not as fortunate as those discussed here, but even in the face of great adversity there was no stopping the spread of mass media.

Leo "The Lip" Durocher being interviewed by Red Barber just prior to the first televised baseball game.

Who's on First?

Formed in 1936, the comedy duo of Bud Abbott and Lou Costello could never have dreamed that they would be inducted into the Baseball Hall of Fame in 1956—and have one of the most popular exhibits, the skit "Who's on First?" This routine was first performed on radio in 1938 on *The Kate Smith Show* and was an instant smash. Awarded a Doctorate of Hilarity from New York University, the duo made their television debut in 1939 on *So This Is New York* and went on to make many films satirizing American life. Much to the delight of their fans, "Who's on First?" appeared in the film *The Naughty Nineties.*

Lou Costello was frequently asked about the skit by fellow comedians and interviewers because they were curious to discover the secret of its success. His response was usually bashful and self-effacing; he would claim that chemistry and hard work are the key ingredients to any successful comedy routine. He also stated that the skit was never memorized or performed the same way twice; instead, he and Bud would seek to outwit and confuse each other, inventing new material on the spot with the intent of keeping the tempo and the skit fresh. Obviously, they were extraordinarily successful.

Les Brown

Bandleader, arranger, and composer Lester Raymond Brown was born in Reinerton, Pennsylvania, in 1912. His musical training included studies at Ithaca College in upstate New York, the New York Military Academy, and Duke University. While at Duke (1935 to 1936), he began leading his first dance band, the Duke Blue Devils. After the Blue Devils split up, Brown moved to New York City and worked as an arranger. In 1938, he formed his own twelve-piece dance orchestra, and through the forties he began his career on radio. He toured extensively, playing ballrooms in leading hotels. "Sentimental Journey" (1944) and "I've Got My Love to Keep Me Warm"

(1948) were two of his biggest hits. In 1947, he began his long partnership with Bob Hope. As Hope's orchestra leader, he toured the world entertaining U.S. GIs for sixteen Christmas tours. Beginning in the fifties, he appeared on television, playing with his "Band of Renown" on the *Steve Allen Show* (1959–1961) and *The Dean Martin Show* (1963–1972).

His version of "Joltin' Joe DiMaggio" is one of the most famous and popular baseball songs ever. Perhaps it was due to the personality of DiMaggio, as well as the exposure Les Brown's Orchestra already enjoyed, that the song became such an outrageous success. Whatever the reason for its success, "Joltin' Joe" is an all-time favorite.

The Wartime Era and Beyond

Born Melvin Allen Israel, Mel Allen began his career at age twenty, while at the University of Alabama, as the voice of the Crimson Tide over CBS affiliate WBRC. In 1936, Allen passed his bar exam and also responded to Ted Husing's invitation to come to New York and audition for him. In 1937, Allen moved to New York as a staff announcer at CBS; he appeared frequently as Husing's assistant, working on the 1938 All-Star game and Series.

In 1939, Allen became Arch McDonald's assistant in New York after McDonald's first assistant called Ivory Soap "Ovary Soap" on the air. When McDonald moved back to Washington, D.C., in 1940, Allen became the principal voice of the Yankees. Luck, talent, and enthusiasm moved Allen from baseball obscurity to the "House that Ruth Built" in less than a year. Allen cheered the names DiMaggio, Mantle, and Rizzuto (whom he branded "the Scooter") and told tales of manager Joe McCarthy's iron fist and volatile temperament. He witnessed the goodbyes of Gehrig (July 4, 1939) and Ruth (June 13, 1948) from Yankee Stadium. Anyone familiar with these events understands that they served as windows into the heart of the nation—powerful moments that moved all who were listening to tears.

Allen was absent from the realm of broadcasting from 1943 to 1946 because of his service in World War II. Other than Bill Slater's and Al Helfer's coverage in 1945, there were no broadcasts of Giants or Yankees games in Allen's absence.

Mel Allen's signature home run call, "Going, going, gone!," is one of many terms baseball announcers added to our language. His passion for the game converted some and outraged others.

Contracts and Sponsors

When Totten, Flanagan, and Quin Ryan began broadcasting in Chicago, they were employees of their radio stations, which meant they worked for and were paid by the station. Any commercial sponsorship was mediated through the station. Most stations forbade their broadcasters to announce over another station. Because most of the pioneers worked as staff announcers, covering sports and other events all year-round, it was unlikely that any announcers would end up moving from one station to another.

Even though Ford Motor Company was paying $100,000 to Major League Baseball from 1935 to 1938, the broadcasters saw no bonus money for the World Series. They received only travel expenses and the honor of the broadcast, and most were grateful for that. Until Dizzy Dean became a megastar on television, the umpires at the games always made more money than broadcasters.

The year 1939 was the first year all major league teams were on the air. At this time, announcers began to be placed under contract by sponsors; Arch McDonald and Red Barber, for example, were signed by General Mills in New York City. Gillette bought the "exclusive rights" to the Series in 1939, and Bob Elson and Barber were the only announcers to cover the event. The era of multiple-network coverage was gone; broadcasting was now an all-out commercial bonanza. It was not until the mid-sixties that the networks gained rights to broadcasts and announcers. Before that time, broadcasters for the World Series and All-Star games were selected by the sponsor and the Commissioner's office, although tradition held that announcers from each team's flagship station would be part of a network broadcast crew.

As the story goes, in 1939 someone asked a labor union man in New York City what he thought the rate of pay should be for the broadcasters of the Series; "thirty-five dollars a game," was his reply. The Series lasted four games and Barber and Elson each received a check for $280—in its generosity, Gillette had decided to double the union man's recommended rate.

When Red Barber moved from Cincinnati to Brooklyn in 1939, he revolutionized the business. He became a "free-lance" broadcaster, complicating the industry and changing it forever.

He worked for the advertising agency representing the sponsor. He had no commitment to the Dodgers even though he was announcing their games. The sponsors changed

over the years, and Barber renegotiated his contract with whatever agency represented the sponsor.

A new wrinkle emerged in the summer of 1945, when Larry McPhail purchased the Yankees. McPhail trumped the ad agency's cards by going directly to Barber and offering him $100,000 for three years and, on top of that, allowing Barber to choose his own assistant. This offer was astronomical at the time—considering Barber had earned less than $150 a month during his first five years in radio—but Barber's share of the listening audience was so large that it could almost be considered a bargain for McPhail.

After the current sponsor, the Old Golds cigarette company, deferred in favor of McPhail's offer, Barber went to Branch Rickey, a personal friend and one of four equal partners in ownership of the Dodgers, to inform him of his decision that he would be moving to the Yankees. Because Rickey knew Barber's value to the franchise and the community, he matched McPhail's offer, and Barber opted to stay with the Dodgers—this time, however, he would be working for Rickey. When Walter O'Malley bought out the other three partners and Rickey went to the Pirates, Barber remained with the Dodgers. The relationship between Barber and O'Malley soon became strained, however, and Barber moved to the Yankees to work for McPhail in 1954.

This story underscores the fragile and unpredictable structure of a medium that was overpowering the nation. Bully tactics by the Commissioner and sponsors disrupted any objective criteria by which broadcasters could be evaluated. What the radio industry faced was a struggle to solidify its own identity and, in many ways, its autonomy.

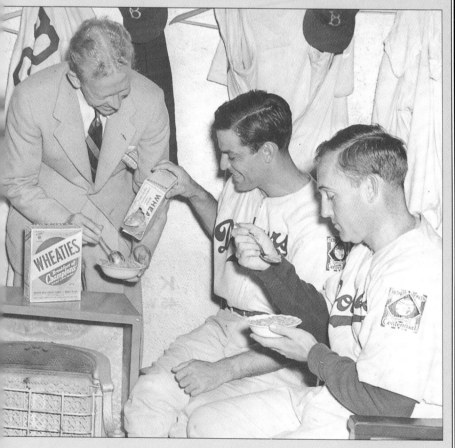

Red Barber (standing) tasting Wheaties with Cookie Lavagetto and three of his Dodger teammates.

In 1945, Larry McPhail, Dan Topping, and Del Webb bought the Yankees for $2.8 million, and McPhail, a colonel under General George Marshall at the time, enacted his own Battle of the Bulge in New York City. He split from the Giants-Yankees broadcasting package, opting for independence and a full 154-game season on the air. His plan called for every inning of every game to be broadcast live; Western Union re-creations would be a thing of the past. Station WINS was secured to carry the Yanks.

All McPhail needed was a voice, and his first choice was Red Barber. Since Barber had been McPhail's man in both Cincinnati and Brooklyn, it was natural that McPhail would want him. Barber was tempted to make the move, but Brooklyn Dodgers president and general manager Branch Rickey matched the offer and reassured Red that he should follow the call of his

Red Barber's "southern hospitality" inspired a generation of broadcasters, many of whom mimicked his anecdotal and sermon-esque style. Brooklyn, the home of Barber's Dodgers, symbolized the American "melting pot," and Barber thrived on its diversity.

conscience (Barber had become a symbol of Brooklyn and was immensely popular in the borough). Barber chose to stay with the Dodgers.

Giants owner Horace Stoneham had made an oral agreement with Allen in 1945 when the latter was on furlough from Fort Benning, Georgia, that Allen, upon leaving the service, would continue as the voice of the Giants.

Unfortunately for Stoneham, McPhail moved quickly and decisively. McPhail had a station, WINS, but he was in need of an announcer, and Allen was the man for the job. After meeting with Stoneham in order to ensure that he was not morally bound to their agreement, Allen was perfectly willing to become the Yankees announcer. From 1954 to 1956, Jim Woods and Barber would join Allen in Yankee Stadium to form the most elegant broadcasting trio baseball has ever known.

New England had been a hub of broadcasting since the early twenties, and in 1939, Jim Britt stepped up to carry on the tradition of frustration for Red Sox and Braves fans. Teamed with assistant Tom Hussey, Britt used his smooth, sparkling wit to bring Sox games to the New England area until 1950 and Braves games until 1953, when they moved to Milwaukee. He covered six All-Star games and two Series on radio, and for NBC television he called the 1951 All-Star game and the World Series from 1949 to 1951.

Teresa Brewer

Known early in her career as Toledo's Miss Talent, Teresa Brewer had a career that spanned decades and chronicled the development of American popular music. As a teen in the 1950s, Miss Brewer had hits with "Music, Music, Music," "Ricochet," and "Till I Waltz Again with You." In 1953 she made her film debut in *Redheads From Seattle,* with Guy Mitchell. With producer (and later, husband) Bob Thiele, Brewer diversified her musical style, recording albums of dixieland, country, jazz, rhythm and blues, and "Vegas" numbers.

It should come as no surprise that Teresa Brewer recorded a popular baseball song, for she was acutely sensitive to America's musical wishes. Her recording of "I Like Mickey" still melts the hearts of all Yankee fans (as well as Mickey Mantle fans); with Miss Brewer's beautiful voice and Mickey Mantle's power and charm, who could resist?

Byrum Saam truly had a gift for gab—his loquacious broadcasts more than picked up the slack for the unproductive Philadelphia A's.

Philadelphia heard Byrum Saam as the voice of the A's and Phillies from 1939 to 1949. In 1938, Saam, the "Man of a Zillion Words," moved from CBS affiliate WCCO Minneapolis to call A's games, bringing life to an otherwise forgettable baseball scene and announcing more losing games than any other broadcaster.

The Texas native started broadcasting football games while at Texas Christian University over their radio station, eventually gaining a spot on the *CBS Football Roundup* in 1935, which followed broadcasting giant Ted Husing's weekly football game. Saam gained national exposure, which landed him a position at WCCO's 50,000-watt station. WCCO didn't want Saam's talents for football, however. Having him do a mock re-creation of the 1935 Series in the studio as an audition, they turned him into a baseball voice. He transferred to the University of Minnesota—he was still a student—and by 1936 was calling Triple-A baseball and college football.

As the announcer for both Philadelphia teams, Saam was forced to call some of the most meaningless games played from 1938 to 1949. Neither of the two Philadelphia teams had even a single player on *The Sporting News* All-Star Team. The only other team in the majors with such a dearth of talent in that era was the St. Louis Browns.

In 1950, Saam became the voice of the A's as the result of a new tack being taken by the sponsor. Before 1950, Saam's broadcast never left Philadelphia; the home game played that day would be aired, usually during the afternoon, and in the evening a re-creation of the game played by the away team might fill out the broadcast time. In 1950, however, Saam's sponsor, N.W. Ayer & Son, an influential advertising agency, decided that Saam and the broadcast team would travel with the A's, thereby calling all games live. The fans received the new policy with delight. The new live broadcasts were much more vivid than even the most vaudevillian re-creation.

Unfortunately for Saam, the Phillies caught fire at the end of the 1950 season and won the pennant—their first in thirty-five years. Over station WIP, Saam's successor, Gene Kelly, called the names of the "Wiz Kids": Curt Simmons, "Puddin' Head" Jones, and MVP Jim Konstancy.

A contemporary of Saam's, Bert Wilson also broke into radio broadcasting of professional baseball via a college station. WSUI, at the University of Iowa, was a pioneer station that featured Wilson broadcasting and singing in 1930. Wilson turned his career aspirations toward sports and moved to commercial station WMT, convincing station management to give him airtime for Cubs home games. This was the beginning of a great friendship, as Wilson sat on a roof out past the center field fence and did the play-by-play.

To his credit, Wilson diversified a bit over time, announcing the Indianapolis 500 in 1941, as well as hockey, roller derby, and Iowa football. Finally, in 1943, Wilson became Pat Flanagan's assistant at WIND Chicago. This was quite a fortunate position for Wilson— the following season Flanagan stepped down and Wilson inherited his beloved Cubs. "I don't care who wins as long as it's the Cubs" was Wilson's motto as he drank up a storm at the mike. A solo act for the Cubs, he remained their voice for twelve seasons, until his career was cut short at the age of forty-four by a heart attack. By Wilson's own

Bert Wilson's premature death in 1955 was a great loss to the radio community—he had brought Chicago to its feet with his animated calls.

admission, his style was developed from famed announcer Bob Elson, the longtime voice of the White Sox, who passed his torch to young Jack Brickhouse, Elson's assistant, beginning in 1940.

Brickhouse became WGN's voice of baseball in 1942, and for forty years he filled the airwaves with his signature "Hey, hey," which brought a smile to the face of the Midwest. Brickhouse called both Cubs and White Sox action and appeared on broadcasts of Series games, All-Star games, and political events, as well as the *Gillette Cavalcade of Sports*. He was inducted into the Baseball Hall of Fame in 1983.

Pitching legend Waite Hoyt (237 victories, including twenty-seven innings without an earned run in the 1921 Series) was the voice of the Reds from 1942 to 1965. Hoyt's impeccable grammar, extensive vocabulary, and

Jack Brickhouse's vivacious style carried the great tradition of broadcasting from the early days into the modern era. William Wrigley's vision of radio as a promotional tool for professional baseball, specifically the Cubs, came to fruition in such talents as Brickhouse.

pedantry combined to dazzle and confuse his audience. Even as a player he was never a "cussing" player, but instead one who insulted with the flair of a schoolmaster rather than a ballplayer.

After retiring in 1938, Hoyt started broadcasting from station WMCA in New York City, sponsored by the Brown and Williamson Tobacco Company. His show, *Grandstand and Bandstand,* featured an eclectic roundup of celebrities, from opera stars to foreign dignitaries. In 1939, Hoyt moved from WMCA to

Waite Hoyt peppered his broadcasts with stories of legends from the era when he was a player.

WNEW to WABC. His goal of becoming the voice of a major league team was dashed when the Yankees signed Arch McDonald.

Down but not beaten, he joined Red Barber on WOR, doing the pre- and postgame shows for the Dodgers. His stay was short, however, because his ambition demanded that he achieve the big time on his own merit. The William Morris talent agency saw to it that Hoyt became the voice of the Reds in 1942. The Reds already had two stations, WLW and WSAI (both of which were owned by Crosley), airing games when Hoyt stepped up to the mike and added a third voice for the Cincinnati fans to tune in to over station WKRC. Burger Beer was the sponsor of WKRC, and the entire Ohio area heard Hoyt conversing and calling the action. Hoyt's solo broadcast was punctuated by a myriad of stories from his experience as a player during the era of Cobb, Tris Speaker, and the Babe.

Some of Hoyt's most memorable clips are about Crosley Field's homey atmosphere. The field stood from 1912 to 1970 and was filled with the ghosts of baseball legends. Moreover, there wasn't a bad seat in the house.

Hoyt's fondness for the past is reflected in the verb tenses he used in broadcasting the play-by-play action. He always called the game in the past tense, that is to say, players *threw* the ball to first base for an out, or

the pitch *was* *thrown* over the plate. Perhaps Hoyt's sensitivity to tense informs us about his attention to the care that should be taken in broadcasting a game.

Jack-of-all-trades Ernie Harwell began announcing in the early 1940s, calling the plays of the Atlanta Crackers in small-town Georgia. Since 1960, he has been the voice of the Tigers.

Top: Russ Hodges (left) and Ernie Harwell (right) worked together to call Giants games. Above: Bobby Thomson's 1951 pennant-winning "shot heard 'round the world" capped a remarkable season for the Giants—in the middle of August, they had been thirteen and a half games out of first place.

Popular Music and Baseball

Baseball and music have a special bond: radio. Of course they competed with each other for the listener's ear but they also merged, sketching American sentiments from the turn of the century onward. For example, "Slide, Kelly, Slide" (1893), by George J. Gaskin, is one of the earliest recorded baseball songs. In October of 1908, singer Bill Murray hit the charts with the second and most popular version of three renditions of "Take Me Out to the Ball Game." Murray's 1903 hit "Tessie" was adopted by Boston's Royal Rooters as their official team song. Also in 1908, "Cubs on Parade" became the first popular recording to use the name of a baseball team. Moreover, folklore tradition claims dance band music had its origins in San Francisco in 1913 when Art Hickman played at the San Francisco Seals' training camp in Sonoma County, California.

With albums such as *Terry Cashman's Greatest Baseball Hits* (1991), composed and performed by Cashman, having songs tailor-made for baseball teams and personalities, it seems the relationship between baseball and music has come full circle. Cashman's song "Baseball and the Braves (Talkin' Baseball)" has become an anthem for television programs and commercial spots.

Russ Hodges became the voice of the New York Giants in 1949 and remained with the club after its 1959 move to San Francisco until 1970. His mellow style and dispassionate tones, with his signature "Bye, bye, baby" home run call, were up-staged by his emotional call of Bobby Thomson's home run off Ralph Branca on October 3, 1951. His call of that moment in sports history—screaming "The Giants win the pennant!"—is one of the most memorable calls in the history of the game. Ironically, Hodges allowed his reporterlike disposition to be buried in the heat of the moment in that 1951 pennant game, blurring his image for many who were not familiar with his regular demeanor.

Russ Hodges' call of Bobby Thomson's famous home run was recorded for posterity by a fan, not the networks.

Dizzy Dean weighed 170 pounds when he was a pitcher, but ballooned to more than 280 when a broadcaster. Whatever his capacity, his audience was starved for more.

Ol' Diz and the Rise of Television

Dizzy Dean, the former leader of the Gas House Gang, became St. Louis' announcer after his arm went in 1941. He called both Browns and Cards games in his typically Dizzy fashion. Runners "slud" and then had to return to their "respectable" bases, players "throwed" the ball, and batters stood "confidentially" at the plate. Don't be fooled by Ol' Diz's down-home way of speekin' to ya; he was as smart as they come.

The "Great One" captured the attention of a depressed country during the 1930s with his mastery on the mound. Families would save all year

The Old Scotchman

Gordon McLendon established the Liberty Broadcasting System in 1949 with its *Game of the Day* program. The games featured on this show were mostly re-creations and were broadcast on as many as 431 stations. McLendon not only was the mastermind behind Liberty, he was the voice behind the re-creations. By 1951, Liberty and Mutual were broadcasting more than one thousand hours of baseball games.

Liberty lasted only three years but it was nevertheless a smashing success for McLendon. It always featured a "hot" game, rather than devoting its schedule to a particular team. Because of this policy, people who listened to Liberty could hear different teams each day. This variety proved very popular, but angered owners and network executives who lacked McLendon's vision and guts. Thanks to Liberty, much of Texas, California, and other western areas were able to receive games.

The "Gas House Gang," shown here in 1934, contributed Dizzy Dean (far left), Leo Durocher (next to Dean), and Frankie Frisch (third from right) to the ranks of radio broadcasters. The spirit and antics of these players helped sports fans throughout the country laugh their way through the Depression.

in order to afford a weekend trip to Sportsman's Park to see the Master strike fear in the hearts of batters with his incredible fastball during the Sunday double-header. The Gas House Gang's reign through the thirties and forties earned them five Series crowns as well as the heart of the nation. They were crass and indignant, throwing dirt at umpires, jeering at fans, and disrupting hotels they stayed in. They formed their own band, the Mississippi Mudcats, which featured guitars, fiddles, harmonicas, and washboards, and in many ways simulated the behavior of today's touring rock bands.

A maverick, and an individual who could only be described as self-possessed, Dean revolutionized sportscasting. He represents an image that networks have attempted to copy again and again, but have never been able to capture. He never worked with anyone else; they always worked with him. At times he was so outrageous that the nation shrieked with delight. He was the first "superstar" of sportscasting. After retiring in 1941, he secured a position with the Cards' sponsor, the Falstaff Brewery, and took to the air broadcasting over WEW (during the day) and WTMV (at night); by August he held the attention of 82 percent of the St. Louis listening audience. Later, he would be heard over WIL and KWK, which were more powerful stations.

In 1944, Commissioner Landis removed Dean from the Cards' Series broadcast because his speech was "unfit for a national broadcaster."

For the 1950 season, Dean went to Yankee Stadium and broadcast with Mel Allen. He was not well received by cosmopolitan New Yorkers because of his act as the irreverent cowboy. Frequent and persistent mispronunciation of names and mangled grammar were his calling card. After his stint in New York, he became Mutual's voice for the *Game of the Day*, and in 1953, he moved into television's first network baseball series, the Saturday Falstaff *Game of the Week* on ABC, which became a huge success. In 1955, the series moved to CBS and Dean had Bud Blattner as his "sidekick."

Blattner, a youngster who claimed the title of table tennis world doubles champion and had also been a meandering ballplayer for the Cards, Phillies, and Giants, took to the network airwaves in 1950, serving as the voice of the Browns. Before that, he had worked on the Liberty Broadcasting System. From 1955 through 1959, he and Dean covered the action for CBS's *Game of the Week* on television. Blattner was overshadowed by Dean's charisma on the air and still marvels at the power Dean wielded from the booth.

Count Basie's Tribute to Jackie Robinson

Recorded in New York City on June 29, 1949, William "Count" Basie's "Did You See Jackie Robinson Hit That Ball?" featured Jimmy Rushing on vocals. There aren't enough superlatives to describe either Basie or Robinson because each man defined the superlatives in his craft. Both men appeared totally at ease while working but nonetheless knew that hard work and dedication were the only means to an end.

Basie died on April 26, 1984, at age seventy-nine. Along with Duke Ellington and Benny Goodman, Basie was one of the preeminent big band leaders of the thirties and forties, and was, in fact, one of the architects of the Swing sound, a member of its royal family. His booking at the Fifty-second Street club called the Famous Door in the forties catapulted Basie and his band into the national spotlight because the club had both national and local radio wires.

The Trenier Twins

Claude and Cliff Trenier began their trek through the music business in Alabama in the 1930s. In the forties, Claude did session work with Jimmie Lunceford and his Orchestra, Barney Bigard, and Charles Mingus. By the late forties, Claude and Cliff had formed their own band and made the transition into rock and roll. They appeared in the rock and roll movies *Don't Knock the Rock* and *The Girl Can't Help It*. Their broad success inspired such groups as the Comets and the Bellboys. In 1958, the Treniers went to Europe as a supporting band in Jerry Lee Lewis' disastrous tour.

One of the most popular baseball songs of all time is "Say Hey (The Willie Mays Song)." To the credit of the Trenier Twins, this tune has been a household favorite for generations.

The End of an Era

The year 1946 saw the triumphant return of baseball to the American scene. All attendance figures of the past were shattered, and radio baseball entered into its true Golden Age. With Allen and Barber in New York, Dizzy Dean in St. Louis, Wilson and Brickhouse in Chicago, and Saam in Philaldelphia — to name only a few headliners—radio had become a part of the game that now was bidding for center stage at the ballpark.

The lean years of World War II gave way to the media explosion we are still feeling the effects of today. RCA marketed the first postwar televisions and the Yankees became the first team to sell broadcast rights for television. The video age was moving in on radio, but before television usurped radio's throne, radio would peak.

The year 1947 brought the long overdue integration of the majors. The game's most competitive league was now truly representative—or at least on its way to becoming truly representative—of the various shades of America. To top this innovation, the Series would make its television debut in Washington, New York, Philadelphia, and Schenectady.

In 1948, Gillette paid $175,000 for exclusive television

The postwar period marked the end of an era; instead of going to the radio for entertainment, families began to gather in front of the television. Today, radio's position in our communities has been almost entirely usurped by television.

rights to the Series and Barber broadcast it. On the radio broadcast was Mel Allen; the time was glorious for all who followed and had come to love these personalities.

Radio is still with us and continues to be popular, but somewhere in the early 1950s, television became a commonplace of daily life, and television broadcasts of sports events replaced radio broadcasts. There was no funeral for radio baseball, but there are many memories....

Memories

The following list of radio "memories" constitutes the radio portions of the material on the compact disc that accompanies this book. Like the book, these "memories" have been organized chrono-

Above: Ty Cobb. Below: Babe Ruth.

logically to present a decade-by-decade sampling of the famous voices and baseball personalities of the time. The songs on the disc are interspersed throughout the excerpts from radio broadcasts.

- The familiar sound of baseball
- Ed "20-Wins" Walsh as a 40-game winner
- Babe Ruth's promise to hospitalized kids, 1929
- The Babe and Lou Gehrig perform a comedy routine
- Carl Hubbell fans Ruth, Gehrig, Jimmie Foxx, Al Simmons, and Joe Cronin, five of the greatest sluggers of all time, in succession in the 1934 All-Star game
- The Babe presents his three goals
- Babe Ruth discusses his retirement, 1935
- George Sisler remembers the Babe's strength in batting practice
- Broadway humorist Senator Ford recalls an exceptional hit by the Babe
- Will Harridge, American League president, discusses the Babe

- A sickly Ruth talks about the importance of getting a youngster started in baseball
- Buddy Blattner's introduction and the 1939 Hall of Fame Ceremony in Cooperstown, New York, featuring Connie Mack, Honus Wagner, Tris Speaker, Larry Lajolie, Cy Young, Eddie Collins, Grover Cleveland Alexander, and Babe Ruth
- Commissioner Landis officially opens the Hall of Fame
- Hank Greenberg at his Hall of Fame induction
- Paul Kerr, Hall of Fame vice president, speaks of the formation of the Hall of Fame
- Ford Frick speaks of the history and future of baseball
- Johnny Vander Meer pitches successive no-hitters in consecutive starts, 1938
- Andy Coply remembers Lou Gehrig as a boy
- Jimmy Foxx remembers Lou Gehrig
- Charlie McCarthy (Edgar Bergen) kids Lou Gehrig
- Lou Gehrig's farewell speech at Yankee Stadium, 1939
- The Hall of Fame induction of Walter Johnson, the "Fireball King," 1939
- Bob Feller's 348 strikeouts in 1946 and his 1938 game with 18 strikeouts
- The voice of Babe Ruth, 1947
- Branch Rickey speaks of the Babe's influence

Lou Gehrig

◆ Jim Farley sums up his feelings about the Babe, 1948

◆ Rogers Hornsby recalls his first year in the majors (1915)

◆ Ted Williams hits a home run

◆ Cookie Lavagetto breaks up Bill Bevins' no-hitter in the ninth inning of the 1947 Series and wins the game for the Dodgers, Red Barber announcing; Mel Allen "blamed" Barber for Bevins' lost no-hitter because Barber broke taboo and mentioned that Bevins had a no-hitter going

◆ Gionfriddo robs Joe DiMaggio of a home run in game seven of the 1947 Series, Red Barber announcing

◆ Babe Ruth, dying of throat cancer, bids fans goodbye at Yankee Stadium, 1948

◆ Bobby Thomson's "shot heard 'round the world," a home run off Ralph Branca to win the 1951 pennant for the Giants, Russ Hodges announcing

◆ Carl Erskine sets World Series strikeout record by striking out Johnny Mize, 1953

◆ Willie Mays makes a sensational game-saving "basket catch" in the 1954 Series

◆ Cy Young speaks of his first perfect game (in 1904) and his first contract (which can be found in the Hall of Fame), 1955

◆ Stan Musial gives a speech at a tribute dinner

◆ Stan Musial's 1955 All-Star game–winning home run and his 3,000th hit, Harry Caray announcing

◆ Paul Waner remembers going 6 for 6 in a 1926 game, 1955

◆ Tris Speaker presents his views on hitting

◆ Ty Cobb talks about creating your own breaks

◆ Don Larsen's perfect World Series (1956) and the Yankee locker room after the game

◆ Jackie Robinson singles, knocking a runner in, to win the sixth game of the 1956 Series

◆ Jackie Robinson recalls troubles when he first entered the majors

◆ Robert Heyland Jr. speaks about his father

◆ Connie Mack speaks about his managerial career

◆ Connie Mack answers a question from a boy about "swearing" in a clip taken from *Here's Babe Ruth*, the Babe's 1940s radio show

◆ Mickey Cochrane remembers one of Mack's mistakes

◆ Mack discusses his eternal hope for "next year's success"

◆ Sid Keener remembers Hornsby acquiring Grover Cleveland Alexander by phone

◆ Frankie Frisch remembers the Mississippi Mudcats (the Gas House Gang's musical group)

◆ Joe McCarthy pays tribute to his great players

◆ Leo Durocher admits he's a genius

◆ Fred Haney receives a testimonial dinner and makes a speech, 1957

◆ Chuck Tanner hits a home run

◆ Eddie Matthews hits a homer in extra innings

◆ Joe Adcock hits his homer

◆ Hank Aaron clinches the 1957 pennant with his 43rd homer

◆ The Braves win the 1957 Series

Bibliography

Anobile, Richard, ed. *Who's On First? Verbal and Visual Gems from the Films of Abbott and Costello.* New York: Darien House, 1972.

Barber, Red. *The Broadcasters.* New York: The Dial Press, 1970.

Bliss, Edward, Jr. *Now the News: The Story of Broadcast Journalism.* New York: Columbia University Press, 1991.

Chandler, Joan M. *Television and National Sport: The United States and Britain.* Chicago and Urbana, Illinois: University of Illinois Press, 1988.

Charlton, James, ed. *The Baseball Chronology.* New York: Macmillan, 1991.

Craft, David, *The Negro Leagues.* Avenel, N.J.: Crescent Books, 1993.

Furmanek, Bob, and Ron Palumbo. *Abbott and Costello in Hollywood.* New York: Pedigee Books, 1991.

Golenbock, Peter. *Bums: An Oral History of the Brooklyn Dodgers.* New York: G.P. Putnam's Sons, 1984.

Jepsen, Jorgen Grunnet. *Jazz Records 1942–1965,* vol. 1 A-B1. Holte, Denmark: Karl Emil Knudsen, 1965.

Kinkle, Roger D. *The Complete Encyclopedia of Popular Music and Jazz 1900–1950,* vol. 2. New Rochelle, N.Y.: Arlington House Publishers, 1974.

La Feber, Walter, and Richard Polenberg. *The American Century.* New York: John Wiley & Sons, 1975.

Larkin, Colin. Guinness *Encyclopedia of Popular Music,* vol. 1. Chester, Conn.: Guinness Publishers, 1992.

Major League Baseball Promotion Corporation. *The Game and the Glory.* Englewood Cliffs, N.J.: Prentice Hall, 1976.

Oslin, George P. *The Story of Telecommunications.* Macon, Ga.: Mercer University Press, 1992.

Smith, Curt. *Voices of the Game.* South Bend, Ind.: Diamond Communications, Inc., 1987.

Sports Encyclopedia. New York: Westport Corp, 1974.

Suehsdorf, A.D. *The Great American Baseball Scrapbook.* New York: Rutledge Books, 1978.

Turkin, Hy. and S.C. Thompson. *The Official Encyclopedia of Baseball* (revised edition). New York: A.S. Barnes and Company, 1956.

Tygiel, Jules. *Baseball's Great Experiment.* New York: Oxford University Press, 1993.

Whitburn, Joel. *Top Pop Artists and Singles 1955–1970.* Mensha, Wis.: Banta Company, 1979.

Zinn, Howard. *A People's History of the United States.* New York: Harper Perennial, 1980.

Index

Photography Credits